Year 1 Poet

Other books by Lori Kane:

Different Office:
Stories from Self-Created, Soul-Satisfying Work Space
(2014)

A Travel Guide for Transitions:
Because Freaking Out About This by Myself
Totally Sucks (2013)

Different Work:
Moving from I Should to I Love My Work (2012)

Year 1 Poet

Lori Kane

Year 1 Poet
Copyright © 2014 by Lori Kane

Cover by: Tabitha Borchardt

All rights reserved. No part of this book may be reproduced in any form by any electronic or mechanical means including photocopying, recording, or information storage and retrieval without permission in writing from the author.

ISBN-13: 978-0-9862996-0-5

Lori Kane
www.collectiveself.com
Email: lori@collectiveself.com

Share feedback on the book at:
feedback@collectiveself.com

Printed by Createspace An Amazon.com company

dedicated to Team Jinda
and to others just now
recognizing themselves
as artists, poets,
and masters of improv

Contents

Prologue 1
Slowing Down 3
    The Morning After 5
    Pickle Recipe 6
    Remember as You Go to
    Change the World 8
    Summer Rhythm 10
    Sneaky 13
    The Art of Neglect 15
    Langley Love Song 17
    Here 20
    Grey Whales at the Beach 22
Loving 23
    New Normal 25
    This Time Love Came Softly In 29
    How We Love 30
    Heal, Banana Peel 32
    How to be Heard by a Total Asshole 34
    The Day of the Playful Heart:
    A Very Important Poem 38
    Even Neck Deep in Shit,
    I'm Glad for Your Company 41
Playing 45
    Low Tide 47
    Ballad of a Flirty Captain 49
    Growing Up on Kingston Drive 51
    If Women Were Pirates 53

  My World Has Blue Dragons 57
  An Ode for Frozen Friends 59
  The Pull of Springtime and the Borg 62

Exploring Identity 63
  Mentor 64
  What Does a Poet Do?
  for Alice Walker 66
  Under Book Covers 69
  Girl's Feet 71
  Fear Asks: Why Create Poetry? 73
  This Is My Work 74
  A Poet's Work 76
  Help Wanted: Poet 80
  Questions for the Gentle 82
  These Words Me 84

Receiving Support 87
Epilogue 88
About the Author 90
About the Illustrators 91
Words are 3-D, Not 2-D and Other Practical Tips for
Being a Poet 92
People on Their Edges Need
Pillow Forts and Other Practical Tips for Being an
Artist 98

Year 1 Poet

Prologue

Last year Daniel and I lived in Seattle. I was a non-fiction book author gathering other people's stories for a living. We lived in a big old house full of kind housemates. I was running a coworking space and helping invent Hopscotch CD – 1.8 Miles of Fun! in the neighborhood. The only real pain in my life was worrying about my mom, who has Alzheimer's disease, and my dad, her primary caregiver. But I was supported and managing: busy and surrounded by friends. I'd walked away from the corporate world to hand craft this life to perfectly suit me. I loved this life.

And then one day, I didn't.

For two months last fall, I barely moved. I didn't want to go anywhere or do anything except watch old Sci-Fi reruns and eat chocolate. Much of my life had become not me anymore, and I had no idea what to do about it. People thought I was depressed. Maybe I was. But it felt more like I was stifled: trapped against a wall. The only way I could hear what I really wanted next was to slow way down, do nothing, and just listen. So I did.

When I began to move again, I didn't know what would happen next, but I knew that I was longing for wide-open space and silence. Both were in short supply in our center-of-the-city neighborhood and life. I needed to be in a place where Daniel, Eva dog, and I could really move. I wanted to live life off leash. We began exploring outside the city and were drawn to south Whidbey, like so many artists and creators before us. In a few short weeks, we bought a house, found people to take over the Seattle house, and we moved to an island. People thought we were crazy. We thought we were crazy.

Still clueless, but now on an island of my own choosing, whenever I sat down to write essays and stories, only poetry came out. It was frustrating and weird. The wide-open space poured into me and my work, and I was completely thrown by it. Lost. Freaked out. Nervous. Angry. And, hmm, a little more free. And a tiny bit happier. I began learning what it takes to listen to silence. To invite silence in.

A few months in, and I still wasn't a poet (I thought then). I had absolutely no idea what I was doing or why. But I wasn't stuck against a wall anymore. I was moving again. I was taking my first eyes-wide-open, shaky steps into a chasm. Into my own fear. Into a deep forest of confusion and loneliness and scary fog. Then one day two new neighbors showed up, having already read my blog. They introduced themselves and said how thrilled they were that a poet had moved into the neighborhood. Holy shit, I thought. I'm a poet.

I used the poems in this book to find my way. Not to find my way out of the fog. Fog, as it turns out, rocks. No, I use poetry to find my way to being content to be right here, present, and creating, no matter where I am, what's happening, or what anyone is feeling. I'm finally free to enjoy being lost. Free to look directly at and rage at the horrible. Free to find and name beauty wherever I want to within the mess.

For me, this book is the first chapter in a poet's story. My story. It's a celebration of what is, right now. It's a reflection on what it takes to remember your artist self, take her hand, and hold her lightly and tightly so you can save yourselves. Plus we tucked in some tips that we learned along the way as emerging artists. Why not? It's scary as hell here at the beginning. Stories help. Poetry helps. Images help. Friends help. And direct clues, from fellow travellers, help too.

Slowing Down

The Morning After

it's easy to love the party
it's easier
still
to love the morning after

so many empty plates
dishes piled high
corks found in corners
furniture askew
memory too
what did I do?

beside sticky counters
trash overflows its cans
and there's pure audacity in that recycle bin
what will the neighbors think?

candles broke their dams
poured beyond boundaries
fell asleep together
in self-chosen shapes

the flowers are relaxing too
hoping to get lucky
their bravest petals off
exploring table tops

relaxing, balloons hover low
more dirigible now
they drift in settled, happy air
find content in stillness

Pickle Recipe

We could argue all day
about what is and is not a poem.
Let's not.
Please keep your perspective.
I'll keep mine.
Let's make pickles in lieu of argument.

in my notebooks
grocery lists and recipes
are tucked among poems
like signposts
for coming back into this body
some days they're my favorite poems

yesterday
two neighbors and I
crafted this one together

Bread and Butter Pickles, double batch:
  50 pickling cucumbers
  10 onions
  4 red bell peppers
  8 garlic cloves
  1 c salt
  6 c cider vinegar
  10 c sugar
  4 TBS mustard seed
  4 tsp celery seed
  1 tsp whole cloves
  4 tsp turmeric

There is so much beauty
in this simple list,
the actions it evokes ---

such love,
history, tradition,
freedom (
we added jalapeños,
eased up a bit on the sugar,
tried four different jar sizes, just because)
friendship
abundance
inspiration (
tomorrow, dills!)

--- that I can't see recipes now as anything but poems.

Feel life itself, poetry.

See friends and enemies as poets.

Find beauty everywhere.

Remember as You Go to Change the World

Remember
as you go to change the world
how amazing that new haircut
plus the kiss of summer's first warm rays on your face
made you feel.

And feeling a little bit better about yourself,
how aware you

became

the sounds

friendly neighbors' gossip
burgundy-black roses
backlit by glowing green
a silent velvet presence
the distant harmonies of birds, insects,
children on swings.

Remember how thankful you were
to be free just then
healthy that moment
moving through space
a conscious being

just

then

The tiniest external adjustment
slightly elevated your insides:
tuning them into the amazingness of now.

This.

This!

This is when you embraced transition, let go, changed.

When you relaxed into being
meltingly aware of the fullness of life.

The moment just after
the hands of a kind stranger
touched your head
and you stepped outside
feeling blessed
lucking into sunshine
feeling Fine on the inside
both changing and changed.

Summer Rhythm

Slow beat
the summer heat
watermelon eat
stop. admire.
earth-hardened feet

eyes at rest
catch warm-air nap
beneath their cap

swim again
just one more lap

that leap
oh that leap

from dock to lake

felt better than crack

remember.
and shivers still
race
down your back.

Selecting sweet berries
by the bucket load

spy rabbit
catch toad

deer stroll past
salad-bar the road

garter snake wake
grass alive under foot
startled dog happy

wag-leaps

won't stay put

tide comes up
surrounds our knees
turns our faces
in, to the breeze,
becoming flowers
to sunny
bumbling
bees.

Wandering summer rhythm
a warm night dance
where bodies come to meet
hot damn
damn

hard to beat.

Sneaky

Do you wonder?
I seem to just keep searching, wondering
shouting "Adventure!"

Magic!
                Mystery!
                                Monsters!
Mayhem
                Real
                                Life

then it's more like "huh? Shit."

I do try to open with the fear

I do

but I'm stumbling shaking
completely lost
moving maybe? ahead

foggy, thinking
then not thinking
testing it out

playing with guessing
messing up and goose
bumps in the night.

I'm really trying
falling failing flailing
angrily, humbly,
trying again

jump back

        freak out

                find

      laughter

            within

Sneaky

When did I accept
open eyes
hands that tremble
a heart alive in my throat

accept all that comes with them,
including, at times, misery?

When did I learn that I Wonder
calling card of trickster Curiosity
holds within her untold endings of
surprise and delight

That she,
in fact, and in fiction
is me?

The Art of Neglect

The difference
between
a thing made by woman
and
a thing found by woman
is seen
in the impact
of neglect.

A thing made by woman
a relationship,
a child,
that unfinished project,
thrives with devoted attention.

A thing found by woman
a forest,
a stone,
that driftwood on the beach,
the cannot-be-finished-by-me thing,
thrives with reverent neglect.

The question asked before

What do I do to make this better?

grew
quite on its own
into

Did I create this or did I find this?

and right now

Does it warrant my close attention
or my holy neglect?

It seems like one begins a quest
of self-discovery
as an individual.

The other a discovery
of the whole.

Langley Love Song

Ferns line the path between
as tall as me
old buildings swoon in the heat
a northern seaside town turned tropical
in uncharacteristically warm May.

Running late to the movies
where women friends wait
I pop into The Star Store
grab sour cherry licorice and some cash
try to hurry back
only to get caught in a warm windless moment
molten feet can only stroll at snail's pace
wonder touches flushing face.

The movie is good
beautifully shot, set in Paris, yet
I'm distracted.

My fingers are still outside
touching tropical ferns just manifest
reading charming fliers meant for tourists
watching pink sea collect orange sky
enjoying the French food breeze alongside Prima Bistro
listening as the checkout woman
carries on three interesting conversations simultaneously
two in person, one on the phone.
Feeling heat upon imaginary bare shoulders
remembering what it feels like to
be sexy and noticed by strangers on the street.

I've always worshipped Prufrock's indescribably lovely
pensive observations,
the breathtaking humanity of his solitary regrets.
He still has no dear women friends, poor man. But I do.
I am not Prufrock today.
Not in Langley.
Not in May.
Here, upon her sweet shore,
I renounce desire for silent sea floors.

We have power beyond imagination here.
You'll rarely to find us cowering in the corner,
choking on the ridiculous.
We don't apologize for our shapes and sizes, our hair,
our thrift-store chic wardrobes.

We have left behind hiding ample arms,
round stomachs, thinning hair
from shallow cavities where human eyes should be.
Have left behind seeing those eyes in the mirror.
We have left behind not dancing.

Come celebrate bunny Monday, movie Wednesday,
farmer's market Friday with us
celebrate spring and summer and fall and winter
appreciate the mouth feel of a well-told story
drive out of your way to find the too-big moon
walk home in magic light on unpedicured feet
smelling newly mown grass with
stunning, crooked noses
on warm summer nights.

We call forth tropical ferns
to a northern seaside town.

We call forth wide mother moon
in her dusky rose gown.

We call forth whales gray, black, and white
with patience, deep roots, beach boots.

We love this place this moment this self this sound.

We are sentient sirens.
Our eyes open in the drown.

Here

I want to be in a place
where
dogs play off leash

where
doors are left open
hearts unlocked

where
neighbors
drop by for no reason.

I want to be
where
responding
to the whims
of weather
of ocean
is natural

where
noticing the curve in the
crockery
the shade of the
seashell
just happens

finding a secret path is
common.

Where
moss and sand
serve
as pillows

where waves and eagles
sing lullabies.

Here.

I want to be here.

Grey Whales at the Beach

gray whales at the beach
and we forget
where we were going
where we are
who we are
people
dogs
even
eagles
instantly transformed
into
giddy
paparazzi

in their presence
pier becomes backscratcher
barnacles good riddance
routine becomes holy
as you are looked into
eye to eye
transported
to Namaste
feel whale shivers in your skin
peace in this place
and you shift
move freer
smile wider whale smiles
breaching the surface
of your former self

walk home craving fish

Loving

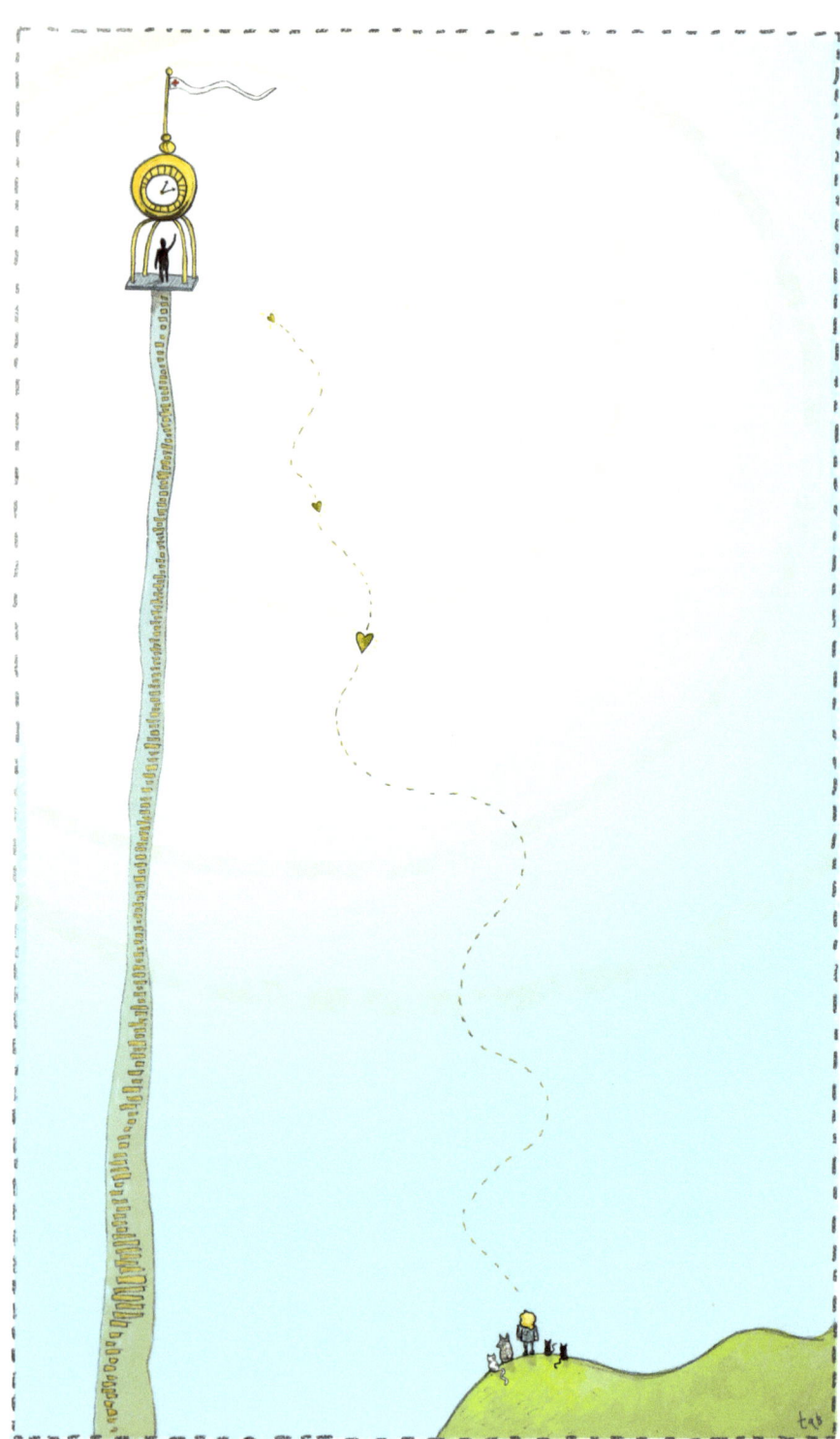

New Normal

You call from the Emergency room
at 5:26 a.m.
assure me that everything is fine
you just woke up
out of breath at 4 a.m.
heart palpitating
in pain.
Being just blocks from the hospital
you drove yourself there
to be safe
but everything is fine.

Everything is not fine!

You have three nurses
all, conveniently, called Chris.
Say you have to go
will call back soon.
I fall back into bed, two hours away from you,
with no way to reach you,
to worry,
feel exhausted from our 5 minute talk.
Eventually drift into helpless sleep.

Wake at 7:30 covered in 3 cats 1 dog.
They feel my fear.
Normally at odds
they'd decided to work together
apparently to physically smoother the worry out of me.
The lower half of my body is numb from their weight.

I begin yet another lecture
about human zones versus animal zones on the bed,
realize their de-stress plan worked,
stop the lecture, hug them instead.

Everything is not fine!

They get it. Move closer in.
You call to say you're waiting on the cardiologist
they are monitoring your blood pressure
(which had been at stroke levels)
every 15 minutes
you will text me results soon.
Assure me that everything is fine.

Everything is not fine!
Our life doesn't work without you.

By 10 you're on meds, feeling better.
Have a follow up appointment with another cardiologist
next Wednesday.
You're complaining now that you don't have Internet access.
The perpetual waiting of the ER dragging.
I relish the good sign.
Text 20 smart things to do to lower your blood pressure.
One at a time.
You text back silly ideas, like "don't wear pants."
I text "These 20 things can be boiled down to one:
    listen to your wife."
Your nurses agree with me.
I gain street cred.
You have to go again.
Assure me everything is fine.

Everything is not fine!
This fucking sucks!
I go outside to throw angry stones into an uncaring sea
cry angry tears down pissed-off-at-life cheeks.

By late morning they release you
you begin the long drive home.
Alone.
Groggy on new blood pressure meds.
Assure me everything is fine.

Everything is not fine!
How can ER doctors know you're ok to drive?!
They just met you. You and groggy don't mix well.

I clean the house to distract myself.
I'm getting no work done today anyway
might as well have a clean house.
Take the dog to the beach to distract myself.
At 3 p.m., as we're walking home, you join us.
I breathe my first real breath of the day.

You tell me about your doctors.
Your medicines.
Your plans.
I nod intently, not listening, and you know it.
I abandon all pretense of being present right now.
Our life doesn't work without you.
What would I do if I lost you?
I feel my artist's skin, stubbornly unwilling to thicken,
begin to bleed with my bleeding heart.

Our vulnerability is so beautiful.

Then I'm back.
"I'm glad you're home," I say.
Remember to breathe again.

We make dinner and I start to relax a little.
Flip on Netflix: Bones, Season 6.
They reunite a kidnapped girl
with parents she hasn't seen in 12 years
using one of her pulled teeth.
We weep. Laugh at ourselves. Move closer on the sofa.

Everything is not fine.

"I thought I was going to die today," you say.
"I thought so too," I say.
"I think I'm going to be extra sappy this weekend," you say.
"Ok," I say.
I don't bother with "Me too" because obviously.

Then the dog and cats join us on the sofa
and everything feels just a little bit sweeter.

I take my third real breath of the day.

Together we take a small step toward fine
embracing to embrace
our new normal.

This Time Love Came Softly In

this time love came
softly in
sitting with my broken heart

last time she showed up
with tea
when I was reading

she arrives beside fear
to demand safe space
to fully feel it

and I've noticed
you and I, friend,
summon her while playing

sharing a game, a secret,
and which Big Bang Theory character
we are

How We Love

We sleep on the floor in the living room with you
when you can no longer use
the stairs up to bed

We hold your head and feed you
when the disease spins lies to your brain
saying that eating is a bad idea

We stop time together
putting the world on hold
to make our brief hours here full, warm, and happy

We invite best friends over to play
through our shared pain
until there is only laughter

And we reminisce
like that time you just knew
how an almost perfect moment could be improved on by
   one stolen sock

We listen closely
past the jagged nagging of our breaking hearts
so that we can hear and know when you're ready to go

Then we sit beside you, telling you how much we love you
through tears, without shame
dragging our sorry selves to a state of rest, peace
so that uber-empathetic you can feel more peace than
   sadness as you leave us

We go home without you
through a bright cold world now hollow
down abandoned streets
to a house that echoes empty

And we begin, without you, to warm ourselves
by honoring you
and through you
honoring ourselves.

You didn't only teach us –
like we thought you did –
the amazing way that you loved your whole life
no

No.

You taught us
how we love

This is how we love.

huh
wow

This is how we love.

Thank you, Grady dog.
Sweet buddy. G-Bone.
Thank you.

Heal, Banana Peel

losing
       every
              thing
now

beginning again

heartache
        sorrow
              going within

birth and her babies
warm toes in the sand
death
and her mourners
cold holding hands

I need absolutely nothing

I sure could use a drink

shattered
        broken
              hope-free
self again in a heap

her tears
       my face
              feeling holy
fell asleep

gift from a daughter
crayons and tea

laugh
drop the crap

cry
drop the act

weightless giggle
start to wiggle

Heal, Banana Peel.

How to be Heard by a Total Asshole

Be quiet for gratitude.
Give yourself time to notice the privileges sent your way.
Not everyone is so fortunate.
When you see how lucky you are, you show up humble.
When you see how lucky you are,
    you can listen and connect.
Lose sight of that and in one breath, one single moment,
    you become the asshole in the conversation.

Today I am lucky for the friends around me, for the earth and sand I walk on, and for the ocean I draw deep healing from.
I am lucky to have access to community, to food, to new ideas and skills, and to resources immeasurable.
I went to bed feeling safe, and I walked down the street yesterday feeling safe.
This body, this spirit, this life – all are a privilege.
I am so unbelievably lucky.
Hello gratitude.

Be quiet for pain.
Sit still long enough to connect with your own pain today.
It's a privilege to have time to sit with your pain. Time to
    share it.
Time to grieve and to heal. Making time within yourself to
    hold space for the pain of others.
Not everyone is so fortunate.
When you hold hands with your own pain, you can sit,
    hold hands with others in pain.
When you move while aware of your own grieving, you can
    recognize grieving and pain – not evil – behind the
    anger, rage, and fear you encounter.
Lose sight of that and in one breath, one single moment,
    you become the asshole in the conversation.

*Today I cry for Amal, my friend helping severely wounded children, moving bodies, daily in Gaza.
Today I cry for the family of my neighbor who died of cancer this weekend.
Today I cry for the family of Michael Brown, burying their son. I cry for the pain I hear in the voices of black parents, Good God I am so sorry, enraged, for the systemic racism that continues to plague our country, and the violence and deaths that arise because so many white people can't see it, let alone have extended conversations about it.
Today I cry for the children of Robin Williams, burying their father. I cry for the stigma around depression and mental illnesses that results in people suffering and dying alone instead of getting help.
Today I cry for my exhausted father, finally admitting that caretaking for my mom, who has Alzheimer's disease, is too much for him. Cry for the man too tired to even pick up the phone to get help.
Today I cry because members of my family—adults I have always looked up to—have turned on each other over the last wishes of my beloved grandparents. That the people who taught me to love can also be filled with hate.
Today I cry about my own helplessness and failures. My failure to share how amazing my Palestinian friends and my Jewish friends are, to talk about how kind and loving my protestor friends and my police officer friends are. My failure to explain how amazing I think each of my family members are to each other, despite our many flaws.
Today, like all days, I cry for the distance between us.
I cry for the loss of connection.
I cry for life extinguished, pointlessly, and far too soon.
I cry for trying hard, when it really matters, and for failing. For the frustration of showing up with tiny hands to shovel a gigantic mountain of crap.
Hello pain.*

Be quiet for joy and humor.
Reflect. Notice the joy and humor sent your way today.
It's a privilege to feel joy, to have a sense of humor.
Not everyone is so fortunate.
Every time you laugh an entire universe of new possibilities opens up.
When joy brings you to tears, a renewed you springs forth, ready for action.
You can bring laughter and joy to others – even these total assholes, right now – when you are in touch with your humor, your joy.
Lose sight of that and in one breath, one single moment, you become the asshole in the conversation.

Today I got to sleep late.
Today is warm and sunny.
Today I get to write something new.
Today a friend made me laugh out loud.
Today I heard my mom and dad laugh together on the phone.
Today I thought about visiting my amazing sister.
Today my dog and cat woke me up by purring in my face
(my dog purrs too, she modulates her growl to mimic the cats
because she thinks purring is so cool, which it is).
Today my friends are laying 2.9 miles of hopscotch path
around our Seattle neighborhood for a gigantic play event this
weekend, an annual neighborhood event that I helped start.
Today I'm having dinner
and seeing a movie with women friends.
Today my husband comes home,
and he's bringing an old friend with him.
Tomorrow we will row out and attempt to catch and eat crabs
in his honor.
Hello joy.

How to be heard by a total asshole…

If you are unable to see how lucky you are.

If your pain is not recognized and acknowledged.

If you cannot feel or even remember joy today.

If you have no time or energy for reflection.

Then you are the asshole in the conversation.

From my perspective, there is nothing else that you possibly could be.

So be the asshole. Bring it. (although for God's sake, put any weapons down first)

And when you find yourself alone, re-listen to yourself.

Be quiet and listen to yourself and hear your perspective, your words. Really hear them. Patiently, as if you were listening to your best friend.

Only an asshole would begrudge you this moment, when you're so far down that you could not possibly be anything else but a total asshole right now.

Hello asshole.

Hello.

The Day of the Playful Heart: A Very Important Poem
For my dear Bernie DeKoven

There once was a heart so playful
it couldn't fit inside its human host,
so it decided to go on a journey.

It became a learner,
studied play,
becoming a teacher,
to play with students.
Learn, learn!

It became a lovable partner,
played with intimacy,
holding hands with laughter
applauding falling leaves.
Sexy, sexy!

The heart created games,
so that others could play too,
then it created a games preserve,
because what the hell else would it do?!

It played with its work:
author, speaker, designer, oh my!
Large-scale play-event inventor!
Eater of pie!

The heart became a parent,
to expand the playful song,
it became a grandparent too,
a whole flock to play ping pong!

And all along its journey,
the playful heart was not alone,
'cause playful hearts kept showing up,
by foot and on the phone,
in through its doorstep,
often in groups,
landing in its Inbox,
hanging out on its stoops!

One day those hearts got together
to honor the playful heart in all
to really effing live it.
They're out there right now, having a ball!

Now every February 1st
both from a near and from afar
we notice our own playfulness
where ever we are.

Go on a mission with others!
Have tea and cookies in your tutu!
Start a game of beach walk bingo!
Or Identify That Doo Doo!

When the heart is playful
The grateful eyes are lit.
Now get thee on a mission.
Tag, my friend, you're it!

Even Neck Deep in Shit, I'm Glad for Your Company

A promise to my fighting family…

> *Today, I will listen, not judge.*
> *Today, I will not trade in a deep ocean of love and respect*
> *for the red-hot coal of contempt.*
> *Today, I will forgive those who appear to judge me*
> *and those who appear to choose narrow self-interest above*
> *love.*
> *Today, when I mess this up*
> *I will forgive myself*
> *and start again.*
> *Because we are worth it.*

I am making the choice today to love all beings,
regardless, actually because, of
our faults and flaws.

We are not united in our perfection: we never were.

We are united in our imperfections.
Wise women say that cracks are where the light shines in:
and, boy, are we cracked.

They say that broken hearts are open hearts:
and, wow, are ours broken.

Yet, it was not before this, it is now—right now—
right in the middle of our own neck-deep-in-fighting-crap
now that we're becoming capable of infinite love.

I am capable of infinite love.
We can love beings
who are bickering, being spiteful,
misremembering, misrepresenting,
feeling contempt, not seeing other perspectives,
not wanting our help, not listening,
sticking their noses into places they don't belong,
lying, stealing, cheating,
and the worst, at least for me:
willfully rewriting a story of wholeness,
removing and forgetting the love,
the complexity that was then, and the sheer simple beauty
that is us, even now.

We're all guilty of these things at some point in our lives.
Forgiveness wouldn't work if we weren't all flawed.

> *Today, I will listen, not judge.*
> *Today, I will not trade in a deep ocean of love and respect*
> *for the red-hot coal of contempt.*
> *Today, I will forgive those who appear to judge me*
> *and those who appear to choose narrow self-interest above*
> *love.*
> *Today, when I mess this up*
> *I will forgive myself*
> *and start again.*
> *Because we are worth it.*

Nasty actions are born from pain,
from fear, and sometimes
from exhaustion.

I believe scared beings, exhausted, in pain,
should be loved,
embraced,
forgiven.
I believe that being loved is
an inalienable right
of the living,
which even includes
the person I'd most like
to punch in the face right now.

This is the way I was raised, family.
You raised me so well
that now my ears can hear
our long and winding story of wholeness
above this moment's name calling.
Now my eyes can see only
tired, sad, or scared humans when I am told
to fear the devil on the other side.
Now my heart can only feel
an ocean of love and respect
for the people who brought me here. For you.
For all of you.

Your story is yours to tell. This one is mine.
In my story you are angels, capable of infinite love now
and you are also a giant pain in the ass, capable of making
me weep with frustration and pain right now.
In my story, all of this is wanted and needed: both angel
wings and ass pain.
In my story, we are made more real to each other, and more
whole, in our brokenness together.

In my story, I would not trade a single one of you crazy people for anyone else on earth.
Even neck deep in shit, I am glad for your company.

If you look in my direction one day and the shit has covered my head entirely
know that unshakeable love for you is emanating outward from somewhere inside that steaming pile.
I am in there thinking of snow ball fights and swimming and fishing and sweet summer salads and songs around campfires.
I am in there recalling decades of your generosity, support, humor, and hugs–for both those who deserved it and those who didn't.
And I am 100 percent certain that when I reach out again one day to find you that your hand will find mine.

Today, I will listen, not judge.

Today, I will not trade in a deep ocean of love and respect for the red-hot coal of contempt.

Today, I will forgive those who appear to judge me and those who appear to choose narrow self-interest above love.

*Today, when I mess this up
I will forgive myself
and start again.*

Because we are worth it.

Playing

Low Tide

Salt thick drips beneath the pier dark wet
hangs in air humid
with seaweed exhausted
driftwood damp
parts, body, of crabs eaten recently
left by birds pirate
who gorge themselves crabbing out of season
without license
barnacles shake themselves
from nose to tail
like a dozen rows purple deep of dogs tiny wet

beach just revealed more mud than sand
like quicksand vile and smelly
will steal your boots
for fun
laugh as you curse
in socks gooey ruined
fall on your butt, fuming
then laughing,
only then notice starfish orange families
humans waterproof and full of humor
basking in sunshine warm and gratitude immense
floating in ebb
feet happy wet

Ballad of a Flirty Captain

I accept responsibility
for floating adrift at sea
everything else I ascribe to luck
Life's not controlled by me.

I fell in love with Mystery first
who often visits here
to experience her argument
for wonder over fear.

I fell in love with Magic next
brought forth by woman wise
crafted raft to follow her
back to paradise.
I fell in love with Ocean then
whose depths I cannot reach
then fell in love with Human Kind
loafing on her beach.
I fell in love with sultry Sun
at shameless first embrace
I fell in love with Sky and Clouds
with Rain upon my face.

And so my ship was caught in tide
while captain flirted with the Whales
left me aground on unknown shoal
no paddle, mot or, sails.

This captain chooses Love and Play,
ahead of Serious Work,
genealogy denying claims to Picard,
confirming surname Kirk.

I accept responsibility
for floating adrift at sea.
But these mermaid fairy pirate friends?
You found me.

Growing Up on Kingston Drive

I remember three tiers of kids:
the teens, not us,
the big kids, us,
and the little kids, our younger sisters, brothers.
the older, as groups,
always trying to ditch the younger,
but as individuals
always up to playing
with anyone at all

willow tree forts
where grownups can't see us
stealing carrots from gardens
like rabbits
that one time, trapped
caught

Magic Terabithia recreated
with twigs and carpet remnants
then stealing away
to the abandoned farm
through corn fields
our ability to find unending treasure
in ruin

demanding
"Go out again!"
to our parents
so our babysitters
who came on horseback
would bring us their horses to ride
pure suburban nirvana

Donkey Kong at Ritchie's house
learning that he liked me
through the awkward gift
of a pen
with all the letters carved away
except for one R
one L
and an &
left between them

Sadly, I liked Kevin

If Women Were Pirates

If women were pirates
ships would smell of jasmine in summer
cinnamon in winter
rain in the springtime
Pirate hats would be more fabulous
Treasure would be friendship,
children and animals and loving this moment

And booty
Oh, that booty
would be
shakin to the music
Every god
Every damn
Every day

When women are pirates
lands conquered
lie within us
Relationships a safe harbor
Fog and mystery a delight,
most days.
Freedom that's found
happens within the chaos
through it, beside it
shakin' that booty
and holding hands

Every sailing
Every away
Every coming
Every home

As more women become pirates
tears flow like rivers
ceilings they shatter
until there is only sky

Abundance is noticed
warm soil between fingers
smooth stones in pockets
cracks allowing in the light
blessed food offerings
the dark warm blanket of night

Vulnerability becomes our beloved worn boots
Gratitude an unstoppable broad's sword
Kindness a golden front tooth
Sharing taken for granted and
Life, not so much

And booty
she'll be dancing
unconcerned with who's watching
Except for your eyes
now known to love pirates
still surprised and delighted
to be here with her dancing

Every God
Every Damn
Every Day

Dragons

North: blue ones
South: orange sherbet-colored
East: with long eyelashes
 that smell of rain
West: tail = sparkling
 overbite = charming

My World Has Blue Dragons

My world
has blue dragons
in the north
orange sherbet-colored dragons
in the south
dragons with long eyelashes
that smell of rain
in the east
and dragons
with sparkling tails
and charming overbites
in the west

Only people
who've been here
a long time

long enough to break open
love deeply

can see them

sometimes strangers
even lean against them
thinking they are streetlamps
or hedges
or sit on them
thinking they are bus stop benches

I just learned
that there are also
tiny purple dragonettes
in the woods
on the island
we just moved to
I saw a picture of one
in a shop
read their stories
in happy hurry

I haven't seen a dragonette
in person yet
we've only been here a month
maybe they haven't seen enough evidence
of deep love yet
I'm working on that
and when it gets warmer
I'm going to walk into the woods
sit in a sun beam
recounting our story
so they know
I'm not a stranger here
I lived here long ago
even before they came
I'm just returning

so they can stop
disguising themselves
as robins now
if they'd like
stop getting chased
off the path
by our dog

An Ode for Frozen Friends

Kentucky is freezing
South Dakota's a mess
New York is frigid
Tennessee's in distress
Maine's streets are frosty
D.C.'s they are too,
and even Ms. Georgia
has frost on her shoes.

It's a confusing time to live
in the Pacific Northwest
Winter's sting feels less harsh now
as we listen to the rest,
for there's no ice here, no snow,
no schools closed for weeks,
no car-ladden ditches,
no frost-bitten cheeks,
no record-low temps,
no politicians spreading blame,
on why it is his fault, no his fault,
ice-covered streets are insane.

We're normally depressed now
into month five of the gray
but this year is different
night versus day
it feels rather warm here
the grass is bright green,
the moss on the rooftops,
is soothing, serene
the sun breaks seem friendly,
the wind's not so bad,
the clouds are quite lovely,
the puddles are rad!

So thank you frozen Facebook friends,
for your tales of winter woe,
you've brought sharply into focus
something important for us to know.
Normally we'd be dreaming
of packing it all in,
moving to Hawaiian beaches,
imagining tropical winds.

It may be dark here in winter
gray land, sky, and sea,
but you've created utter delight here this year
about 48 degrees.

The Pull of Springtime and the Borg

bees
up to their knees
in swollen pollen
tulips rise
kiss the day
apples blossom
giggle, blush and
run away
frogs harmonize
in undirected choir
damp soil winks
to beckon seed
earth preens
her baby greens
nudges buds
from ground's nest
puddles twirl
feet to lure
a slow first dance
in shorter pants.

spring,
the first and better Borg,
arrives
in warm rain ship
with heart beat engine
a teetle a tootle
resistance is futile.

Exploring Identity

Mentor

My neighbor saw her drown a heron in 10 seconds flat
then with her partner strip it bare, a feast of flesh
moments later bone

that shook the tendency to romanticize her out of my
fingers, also bone

I watch the eagle work
focused head
forward beak
eyes seeing God knows what
silent and alone

Her boathouse landing makes small birds rise
some angry and annoyed by her presence
they don't faze her
eyes never waver from the ocean rolling gray
strong and steady, waiting
unapologetic for hours at work her play

The dive when it comes is faster than expected
                          precise
quiet at a distance then surprisingly loud upon approach
your ears feel weight, like a small jet engine

Her work brings awe
to be present to bear witness
plus some dread
imagination fully engaged, I am a clue-free fish
here one moment, dinner the next, dead

Does she give thanks, I wonder, and does the fish?

Somehow I know she does

She has the time.

Her presence keeps me wondering in earnest
if I'm truly fit for this wild place
this life

she helps me hear my answer too
repeatedly
bone-certain
Hell yes I am.

What Does a Poet Do?
for Alice Walker

Do you know
that writers
our hardest moments
fought in quiet attic battlefields
come sit with you
to weep with joy?

Do you know
that humans
at our most afraid
carrying hearts beyond tender
act
because your voice
gives us faith in ourselves?

Do you know
as yet another person
loses sight of humanity
taking precious life
precious limbs
taking almost everything that matters
pointlessly
again and again and, fuck, not again,
until I want to rip the American
and, this month, Earthling badge
off my burning human uniform
hurl them into dark forgiving space
submerge my inner being down into deep quiet waters,
when I need to hide,
do you know I turn to you?

When I lose the will to continue
feel helpless, certain
there is nothing I can do.

In that moment
this moment
Alice
I find you.

Thank you for showing up every day
bravely answering your question
my question now too.

What does a poet do?

Under Book Covers

Drinks with friends
talk turns to Amazonian best sellers
what we read when no one is watching:
murder mysteries, sci fi, poetry, and smut,
oh god, the smut

tales circulate
of $30,000 made
roughly 30 gazillion dollars in indie writer land
on one monster erotica book
WTF?!

Wouldn't be so terrible,
said shoulder devil,
to write sex and trashy romance
to splash rock-hard abs
onto front and back covers

writing
hard and fast

screaming "Oh God, FUCK the font!"

hair blown back in creative collaboration

until we're exhausted
damp
satisfied with sales
and more than just a little embarrassed?

I was certain
from ages 10 to 43
that this was selling out.

Today I'm not so sure.

Maybe this is just skinny dipping writer selves

leaping
all in
feet and cover-abs first

guns blazing
chest bare
exposed

utterly delighting in
being delighted in.

Maybe being human
isn't so bad
after all.

It's time to start creating
what we really
love.

Girl's Feet

poet, artist   find the space   your place
outside the race   where
mind goes empty
ego floats to grace

go there every day   no matter what   every day
if only for a moment
Go there   Go there   Go

There now.
Can you feel the earth? Her spinning rhythm?
Feel your strong and calloused feet
moving toward water like water
carrying her own back to family

notice your own arrival at the place with empty vessel
the dipping into water
the scooping up of another world
notice your own return
with glowing face
supported on strong back and shoulders
dripping abundant life for you
for beloved others
balanced on your small frame

Return   Release   Repeat

you hold within you now
the strength of a thousand oceans
relax and feel the beat
in those perfect
dusty feet
your
girl's feet

Fear Asks: Why Create Poetry?

Fear asks:
why create poetry
when there's no apparent
market for it?
In response
I craft an ocean of poems
dive deeper into
our quality and quantity
our silliness and seriousness
our purposeful purposelessness
our playful connection and disconnection
simultaneously.

Go ask bees:
why all the fucking honey?

I'll stay here
swimming in poetry
until they feel the need
to justify creation
of their own
sweet healing gold.

This Is My Work

Something snapped inside of me.
I can only do soul-satisfying work now
alone, and with people I love.

I've been apprentice
to the phenomenon
for roughly ten years.
And find it has more to do with
community support
expanding love
ceding control
appreciating freedom
recognizing instinct
bowing to curiosity
visible foolishness
laughing our asses off together
shattering visibly
reliable magic
and flowers left on luck's glorious flaky altar
than it does with being picky about
exactly what gets done
who shows up
how I am compensated
what my title is
and everything else
I thought I should care about.

Fuck Should.
In my world
this being here
this learning what actually matters
is the work.

A paying close attention
to the experience of our being

offering it back to God or anyone else at all
as a gift
with as much gratitude, surprise, delight,
personally curated foolishness

as we can muster, manifest, admit to

This is my work because it softens me.

By the time I'm 90
I will be a downy warm blanket
or puppy's tummy
for all the hands that touch me.

This is my work.

It's time to start doing it without apology.

A Poet's Work

the beginning usually sucks:

unlearning truths
undoing selves
unending days
unwending paths

good god, that's total crap.
Then what?

self laughs at self,
or cries,
ceding the stage
ego averts
smiles in her eyes
moves down to find her seat
audience complete

enter wonder
stage left
then pirates
magic
lowered on ancient ropes
by work-worn hands

open-mouthed
awe-struck
watching that fog blanket
move along the water
alive
and so remarkably well
alone and playing
under a Scooby Doo moon

        rediscovering drift
           wood remossing the way
               every moment wanting a coffee cup
                every thought taking a day

as audience
kind eyes fail to see
on purpose without purpose
playing along
letting go
until one with the show

wading through
clouds boots
sandy with thoughts

        successful
          this moment
            at silencing ought's

at making space
at stopping

at breathing
with ocean lungs

at peering out eagle eyes
above beaked shrieking noses
the slightest shifts in surface
hinting at mysteries below
and also, just dinner,
fish

at times unabashed
pirates lusty
for warm
wanton
words
spilling
like
candy
piñata
rain

We'd rather eat lichens
than toil
in a story
of someone
else
's
making

might not seem a good living
but usually is

a poet's work ain't never dun

yet almost always
by the end

she's clapping her hands

laughing along

utterly surrounded
by friends,

crying,
amazed

by the
breathtakingly
beautiful
pirates

who let
themselves
in

Help Wanted: Poet

Work begins
with fed cat
on the windowsill
butt in chair

Ears perpetually tuned to TWBS,
the wind and bird station
even during the big meeting
especially within the mundane

Good work for pirates
with tied-in-person tongues and agile fingers
who delight in looking silly on paper
lighting the fireplace with old resumes

Good work for the remarkably interested
in everything
and the remarkably bad
at caring about when they showered last
or brushed their hair
or teeth

Good work for souls inclined
to bow before nature
and stand up
to words
For those deaf to the labels
pretentious,
self-centered, and
pointless,
except when the page itself
softly nudges delete

Good work for hearts
sometimes embarrassed
by how much they love
stunning broken places
glorious piecemeal selves

Good work for those
with gratitude unshaken by humans
most days,
yet rattled, able to move in a flash,
when the dog farts.

Finds wild peace within rivers
within the wandering
the wondering
the longing
the looking on.
Within the never knowing
the wading in slowly
and the jumping
all in

Rarely prepared
always surprised and delighted
when the whole bloody mouthful
falls away
into
grace.

Apply within.

Questions for the Gentle

How did you do it my ancestral poets? How
did you feel this world so completely, when
the gentle and the kind suffer, while
the greedy and mean run so many things?

How did you embrace this world, where
war in all its forms spreads like fire, where
self-delusion and distraction trump noticing, where
exploitation, rape, and weapons are just good business?

How do you do it, girls
crouched and running through the rubble? Parents
burying found pieces of your children?
How do you give anything more, when
so much of you has been taken, when
fear, rage, and despair are your closest neighbors, when
you cannot muster even the smallest desire to reconcile—
not even for your God?

How do you do it
sisters and brothers? How
do you stay with the terrible yet hold on to the gentle? How
do you turn an open face into the horror yet also replenish
your soul? How
do you thrive while holding so much pain?

I'm actually asking.
Fuck poetry.

Today I am so drained by what I feel
that I stand stuck, muddy,
exhausted, almost motionless. Holding
nothing more than my own heartbeat, creating
nothing more than my own self,
softly, from within.

These Words Me

I look forward to being dead.
The magic moment that poets —
life's painfully literate jesters —
become cool and wise:
labels most of us can't fully live our way into.

I look forward to seeing
my life bookended,
parentheses complete:
Lori Kane (1970-2070)
(For example, people, I'm in no hurry.)

I look forward to being words
on a page.
Nothing more.

To laughing in the knowledge
that just-words me
never again has to decide
what to wear.
I am words now!
Cover me as you please to suit your needs.
I am outside
within the field of imagination
running barefoot through the grass.
I am the grass
tickling your bare feet.
Come find me in laughter
within tears on cheeks.

I look forward to a graceful awkward kid
happening upon me these words,
thinking better of herself
for having found me,
learning to trust his
solitary and collective self,
while standing on nothing more solid
than loosely gathered stones
in pockets.

I look forward to being present when you realize
that you can be words!
(or some equivalent love)
an entirely different something
than what you've been told
you must be.
Like Robert Frost,
Emily Dickinson,
and T.S. Eliot
were for me.

I look forward to sharing tea
to giggling as you rush
to save pages, screen, or keyboard,
from a spilled liquid
that cannot truly touch me.
I love stains and wrinkled pages!

I look forward to comparing footnotes with friends,
to hand-scrawled notes around me,
expanding ourselves,
within anthology
our collective infinity
just you,
our other poet friends,
and these words me.

completely

free

Receiving Support

Poetry taught me to look between the words that fall and stick to the wet grass of the page. To find/take/give comfort there, too. Thank you, poetry. Thank you, poets.

Between the words are my close friends, family, neighbors, and environment. This work wouldn't be possible without a large gang of helpers, supporters, friends, improvers, head-clearers, cheerleaders, and get-off-your-butt movers.

Husband Daniel, who makes up for my differently wired and technology self-blocked brain. He allows me to be responsible only for what I love—the words, the people, the wandering, and the gathering together of the pieces. From that gathered collection of bits to actual book, he does the rest. Amazing. Thank you.

My friends Tabitha, Bas, and Bridget, the illustrators, who helped me better understand that every pair of eyes, every heart, finds a different thing within a poem. How wonderful a gift is that? Words fail. And Tab's amazing book cover. Wow. I'm in awe of your magical skills. To me that's what you all are: magic. Thank you.

My friend Kathy, who edits patiently and quickly for quirky, fails-to-plan-ahead-because-Ooo-that's-a-cool-rock me. And for reminding me of the teaching capabilities of birds. Book #4. Thank you, again.

And all the rest of my family, friends, and neighbors. The life bursting forth within my work I find within you. Without you, I'd be connected to humanity mostly in my head, instead of in real, flesh and blood, laughing and eating and crying together ways. The strongest poems are those with the strongest direct ties to you. Thank you.

Epilogue

I'm a poet. Through joy and pain, this thread runs through me. I'm not getting trapped within the eddies of my own fear like before. Not for long anyway. I'm a river. I keep moving. Poetry is my heart dancing. Some days, weeping.

If you came here looking for perfect poems, bless you. May you find them one day. This book elevates flawed work. Individual pieces aren't perfect, and yet as a collection, I hope they make visible the seed and DNA of an awakening poet, an artist. Visible heart. If you thought, for even one moment, "I bet I could do that," you're right. This book is for you. Our world needs more poets. More artists. More people with heart, not just skin, in the game. More you.

Today Daniel, Eva, and I are islanders. The nearest town has more rabbits than people. I'm living without housemates for the first time. We take long walks, watch deer and eagles, gather driftwood and stones, pick apples, make gifts for neighbors, and put up a basement full of food for the winter. Daniel and I are hosting workshops here at the beach now too. At 44, I recognize myself as an artist, a creator, a poet. The last time I suspected this I was 13. It's more scary and magical today. Steeped in silence now, my work has synchronized itself to the movement of the tides and the changes of the seasons. They're my coworkers.

The sections of this book surfaced when I re-looked at eight months of my poetry. I noticed patterns in where the poetry came from and then patterns within the poetry in each of the sections. I became a poet by slowing way down, noticing what I loved (thank you both play and pain), and loving who/what I loved more deeply. By playing more often, exploring greater depths of my own identity, and by receiving more support from my friends and family than I'd allowed myself to accept in the past. How do I know this? The poetry told me so. The real process was not orderly like a book. I/it/we were a mess. The true order of emergence can be in seen in blog archive at www.collectiveself.com.

There are all kinds of bravery in the world. Poetry is my kind. The question Year 1 asked was simply this:

Are you an artist?

My answer—a quiet, invisible certainty moving deep within a dark forest of uncertainty—Oh, hell yes. I am. Maybe we artists have to walk into the forest alone, I don't know. But that's not going to stop me from saying out loud what I wish I'd heard sooner:
Join us!

As scary as it is to be an artist, there's nowhere else like it if you have an artist's heart. This is home. This is where we make our quirky worlds real, which is hard but far easier than trying to remake ourselves to fit, again and again, into a rigid world that just doesn't get us. Nowhere else will we find companions who adore us instantly as we are. People who help us find contentment within chaos. That's our job, artists. That's what we do. We bring forth new worlds. We bring forth contentment in chaos. And we stare into the eyes of horror, of hell. Not to die, like soldiers, but to record, remember, for the hearts that must look away for now. For those who will one day need to come back, revisit, remember, and start again. We are makers of curious, broken, clue-filled maps that broken, curious, and awakening hearts will follow. Including, visibly and inevitably, our own.

– Lori
November 25, 2014, Whidbey Island, WA, USA

About the Author

Lori Kane is a poet and writer who loves to wander. She studies transitions—foggy, messy, chaotic, lovely in-between places—by collecting stories from thriving and struggling ordinary humans, writing poetry and stories and essays, gathering rocks and driftwood on beach walks, and being an active part of an Alzheimer's disease improv troupe caring for her parents.

Lori lives on Whidbey Island, Washington, USA with husband Daniel, Eva the dog, and Joe, Bella, and Batman the cats.

To find more of Lori's work, visit her Collective Self website at www.collectiveself.com, stop by for a chat on her Facebook author page, or follow her @CollectiveSelf on Twitter.

Photo by Daniel Gregory. More of his work can be found at www.danieljgregory.com.

About the Illustrators

Tabitha Borchardt, a.k.a "Funkisockmunki," is a recovering graphic designer turned illustrator-weirdo who spends most of her time cultivating a garden, drawing, arranging sticks and rocks, and talking to trees and crows. She resides in the Pacific Northwest surrounded by as many plants and rainbow-emitting devices as she can get her hands on. Tabitha's work appears on the cover and on pages 12, 16, 24, 48, 72, and her self portrait on this page.

Bas de Baar is a writer who draws. He loves to make visual maps and travel guides for the collaborators of our brave new world. Bas lives in The Netherlands. Bas' work appears on pages 50, 55, 56, 61, 83, 99, and his self portrait on this page. See more of his work at Basdebaar.com.

Bridget Beorse is an art maker and wilderness explorer. Her current projects include murals, illustrations, graphic design, and traversing the temperate rainforest. She lives in Seattle, Washington. Bridget's work appears on pages 4, 39, 46, and 68. See more of her work at beorse.squarespace.com.

Words are 3-D, Not 2-D and Other Practical Tips for Being a Poet

Many common writer-centric writing tips—great advice—don't necessarily stretch deep or wide enough to work for poets. I found that I had to create my own addenda set of tips for myself this year. Here are ten...

1. Writer tip: Know your audience.
   Poet tip: Become your audience. As creator and audience, you are more, you have a wider and deeper perspective, so you naturally see more of what's happening. You have more time to see what you, and those in the seats beside you, really love most. The fluid movement from creator to audience to creator again, with time, is what allows us to get better at focusing on what matters most and letting go of what doesn't. You can see me notice this happening in the poem A Poet's Work.

2. Writer tip: Never use the passive voice when you have the option to use the active voice.
   Poet tip: Don't tell a poet *never*: we know it's not true. Trust the voice that's speaking through you. Use whatever voice you want to, speak the words out loud, and refine until the poem sounds like you. Some days you're passive. Spend the time to understand why your ear wants what it wants, what choices several poets you respect would make, and be able to articulate why you made the choice you made.

3. Writer tip: Write every day.
   Poet tip: Play a little every day. I tried to write poetry every day, failed, felt bad about myself. Then I noticed that poetry is actually play. My favorite kind: the scary, visible, on-my-edge, thrilling kind that is work/play. For

me, reading, gardening, going to movies with friends, walking on the beach, walking the dog, cooking and food preservation, wandering new places on foot, and playing games are also play. So I created the tip Play Every Day to stop feeling bad about not writing every day. Lo and behold, today I write poetry almost every day, for the fun of it. A little blurb in a notebook, some micro poetry on Twitter or on the back of a grocery receipt, a drafty draft on my Facebook page, words written on rocks, or drawn into the sand, or into dirt on car windows, or a pulled together draft poem in my blog. I also now catch beautiful or striking phrases in people's everyday speech and think or say, "Ooo, that's a poem." For me, roughly 80% of poems emerge from play and the other 20% from pain. Every poem in the Slowing Down and Playing sections of this book, most in the Exploring Identity section, and two in the Loving section are the direct result of play.

4. Writer tip: Take a pen/notebook/recording device with you everywhere you go.
   Poet tip: Relax. You are Source material. If you often leave home forgetting all 10 of your documentation devices, you might be an artist. Don't worry about it. Some ideas are meant to be lost. Other ideas will follow and find you no matter how many times you forget your pen. Poet, you don't need perfect notes, stacks of transcripts, hours of audio and video footage. Hone yourself as device. Play the Recall the Feeling game. As you walk or sit in a place, tune into the unique feeling of the place. What does it feel like here? Use all your senses. What does it smell like? What does the air feel like on your skin? What can you hear? What triggers the feelings you and others have here? Play this game for even three minutes and you'll have plenty to say when you get back to your writing tools. Play this game with another artist sometimes too to see how the game changes.

5. Writer tip: Organize your thoughts before writing.
   Poet tip: Do whatever activity feels right each day to empty all thought from your head before writing poetry. Start as wide open and empty and receptive as possible and end as wide open and empty and receptive as possible. Writers are like human bodies: they have complex systems to feed their work and to remove waste from their writing. Poets are more like sea sponges: simple creatures that allow a constant flow through their open bodies to feed them and also rid them of crap.

6. Writer tip: Stay up to date on good grammar.
   Poet tip: Follow sound, rhythm, curiosity, and intuition to whatever scary places they take you: even down strange language alleys and to your own edges. For example, many excellent writers, including my mentors, pooh pooh adjectives and adverbs in the way that 10-year-olds pooh pooh big preschool DUPLO blocks now that they've moved on to more complex LEGOs. I secretly love them (adjectives, adverbs, mentors, and DUPLOs). So I thought, "What would happen if I just changed where all the adjectives live in a poem?" The result was the poem Low Tide, which I will love forever even if nobody else does. Being at your own edges is weird and hard and good. It's here that the person I most need to learn with next as an artist finds me.

7. Writer tip: Hire the best editor you can afford to perfect your work prior to publishing to a wide audience.
   Poet tip: Share written and spoken drafts with a wide unplanned swath of humanity, plus at least one animal, tree, body of water, and the sky when you can. And. Work with a few trusted people who love you, stretch you, and will forgive you (and you them) as needed. If you trust poems in their evolution, then faith in yourself (tough for artists, always) becomes less important. Poems will listen to good ideas wherever they come from and ignore bad ones wherever they come from. Poems

evolve with time and are never really finished. They teach us: are smarter than we are. Prior to a big publication, like a book, have another poet who loves your work read your work and provide feedback. If you don't know any living poets who love your work, read the entire body of work of a few dead poets you love and then channel them to review your work. Dead people who inspire us give the best feedback. For the non-poem parts of your major publications (like this), have a dear editor friend edit the work. Ideally the friend is 100% trusted by you to the point that you review edits for the purpose of learning, not to argue (much). If you don't have an editor friend this close, work on finding one. As a writer-turning-poet you need an editor who loves you more than ever before—one willing to patiently listen to a sea sponge and then perform sea-sponge-to-human translation as necessary and with an open, loving heart. If you're not enjoying the process, keep looking for more compatable partners until you all love the process. As time passes, be willing to shift roles, or say goodbye, to maintain friendships when you no longer love the process like you used to.

8. Writer tip: Use the right word, not its second cousin. I've heard that Mark Twain said this.
Poet tip: Frame this quote and hang it on a wall near where you write, set it as wallpaper on your devices, and/or have it tattooed on your forearm. Treat "right" like it's forever. And also know that it's actually not forever. Unlike other forms of writing, poems are never finished. Small, portable, and useful muses, poems may find themselves published again and again. So poets get to spend their lifetimes searching for the right word. A poem may find a better "right" word 20 years later and breathe new life into itself. If you like the idea of spending your lifetime looking for the right word, you might be a poet. If you like the idea of

spending your life with a second cousin, you might be a redneck. Whoops, my heritage is showing.

9. Writer tip: Read a lot.
   Poet tip: Listen a lot, watch a lot, participate a lot. Listen to spoken word poetry, song lyrics, dialogue, and speech patterns in the street. Listen to your own work out loud and to the voices and silences of nature. Go to poetry readings, music concerts where lyrics are involved, spoken-word street performances, screenplay and script read-throughs, and plays when possible. Go to places where people chant words. Go to protests and picket lines where people shout words together (and lend a hand while there). Listen to poets on YouTube and at poetry readings and anywhere else they are speaking their work. Then go where it's silent. Listen to wind, water, birds, rain, trees, and fog. You have to learn to listen to white space, love emptiness. Can't find silence? Make your own. Listen to the rails beneath the train, to the concrete pattern under bike or car tires, to the quiet rhythm of your feet on the ground. Meditate. Attend a silent meditation retreat where only notes can be passed, no spoken words can be used. If you're in grade school, recess works great for this. In high school, detention works great for this. Use your feet. Move to where you can listen. Absorb.

10. Writer tip: Don't use a long word when a short word will work.
    Poet tip: Words are 3-D, not 2-D. Don't sell any word short. Economy within words and poems is often a good thing, and sometimes not, depending on what you're doing. I think of words now like I think about plants in my garden. You are within your rights to choose a plant based on just one thing: Oh, pretty flowers! But for lasting rewards and benefits look more closely. For example, choose a plant because it has edible bits, attracts wildlife, will love the spot you have for it, provide shade

for another plant that needs it, needs only the water the sky in your area will provide so you won't have to mess with it much again, will have a symbiotic relationship with the plants around it, and is beautiful in its own unique way, especially in context. Go deeper. Roll a word around in your mind and on your tongue and peer into it like trying to peer into an opaque marble. Notice its sound and shape, the weight of the word, the various meanings it has, the feelings and memories it evokes, what it does to the movement of the line or stanza or piece, and its relationship to the other words around it. If it also happens to be a short word, good for you. You may have just widened your audience.

People on Their Edges Need Pillow Forts and Other Practical Tips for Being an Artist

"Say no more often than you say yes. Guard your precious time, which will almost always make you feel like a huge jerk. Bail on social networks, fashion, op-ed, television, workouts, diets and shopping or anything else drumming the voice of mother culture into you at the expense of your humanity. Bail on anything or anyone that wastes your time and talent by stealing your love for the world and yourself and go pursue your weird and wonderful human side."
- Tabitha

"Just because the masses don't yet see the wisdom in slowing down, saying no most of the time, going within, and utterly surrounding yourself with plants and bunnies and crafting and home repairs to nurture your artist self, doesn't mean it isn't deep wisdom. To me it means you're on the cutting edge. Brave. A leader in the task of recreating ourselves from the inside out and on our own quirky, kind, and more lovely terms this time." - Lori

"I definitely didn't realize starting out that making a successful career doing art would require so much: marketing, business planning, tax rate calculating, and sigh, math. That's not why I went to art school! What I've learned, though, and my own advice I'd like to share, is that it's necessary to treat finished art/writing/creative works as marketable products to use them to pay the rent. Take a small business class!

Learning to effectively market myself and budget myself allowed me to actually reach people who wanted to pay me and understand how much to charge so that I could eat. It also sidesteps hurt feelings that come from negotiating the worth of your art in dollar amounts. When I know that I'll be able to pay for today's sandwich, and tomorrow's, I can more effectively focus on making a great piece of art. Being better at business lets me get through the money stuff faster and get back to the creative stuff." - Bridget

"I asked Bas if he had anything wise to say to emerging artists here at the end of the book, and he sent me this drawing, without explanation. I'm not sure what it means. At the very least it means don't ask a cartoonist to write you a paragraph. The second lesson I took from it is that a wolf in a chicken costume should remember to shave his legs. But I suspect it says much more. Like a Zen koan. Keep looking. Keep wondering. Go deeper. Thank you, my silly Dutch Budha." - Lori

"I spent a lot of time worrying about not pulling my financial weight in my relationship with Daniel after I left Microsoft and refused to go back to the large-scale corporate and academic worlds. I don't anymore. Not since I noticed how much what I'm doing is helping him and those around us. Not since I noticed that not doing what's expected of us is the harder work I'm here to do. Most days I'm the one who he looks to when he needs to figure out a new way to be brave, or how to hold on gently and tightly to what he loves most about himself against fear and doubt, and, more recently, to see how to be an artist." - Lori

"Don't listen to any distant voice that says an artist's work is worthless, pointless, or easy. Even if you never sell a single piece across your lifetime, that's total bullshit. We are changing ourselves regularly and visibly. We follow our artists' hearts into places we and others fear to go, staying on our own edges. We're not seen by anyone else for long periods of time when we work, so we have to be brave. We must work together or almost nobody will see our work and we won't make a living, so we have to be collaborative. And even when we work together, we work alone, so we have to be self-reliant. It's not easy here. People on their edges need pillow forts. When we are touched by a Wow-for-us artist's work, it can't be enough just look at their work. We have to connect as people. We have to ask if we can peek inside their pillow fort or invite them into ours. So we can keep growing and recreating ourselves, our world."
- Lori

www.ingramcontent.com/pod-product-compliance
Lightning Source LLC
Chambersburg PA
CBHW041805160426
43191CB00004B/61